# How to be a Modern Princess

quadrille

Meghan Markle has changed the rules. What was once a seven-year-old's unattainable dream has now become an achievable reality for everyone. Step into Meghan's glass slippers, and find out all the ways in which you can channel your inner modern princess. Simple yet profound, this humorous little book could change your life forever. Read it, enjoy it, learn from it… and it's just possible that your fairy tale dreams *could* come true.

Get everyone to call you
by your middle name.

Be a fashion icon.

Learn calligraphy; nice handwriting
is a must for any princess.

Follow your heart in all things.

Always wear labels that *have* to be Googled.

Be outspoken, but not brash.

Perfect the art of gazing adoringly
(into the camera / your prince's eyes).

Mix stylish on-trend looks
with timeless Hollywood class.

Ditch texting. Go old school
with hand-written notes.

Get a cute rescue dog and
give it an even cuter name.

Be an actress.

Don't shy away from a Royal PDA.

Be both interesting and interested.

Get friends in high places –
who needs Tinder?

Land a feisty role in a hit tv show.

Get divorced (sorry Wallis Simpson...)

Be a feminist.

Get a cool paralegal alter ego.

Be glam at all times.

Become 'editor-in-chief' of
your own lifestyle brand.

Get the princess glow;
drink green juice, lots of it!

Make Pilates your workout of choice.

Celebrate being a woman.

Celebrate other women.

Remember, lunch isn't lunch
without something sparkly –
in a glass or on your finger.

Focus less on wearing glass slippers and
more on breaking through glass ceilings.

Never forgo morning coffee –
it's a photo opportunity, obvs.

Expand your horizons;
travel to far-flung shores.

Develop a palate for fine wines.

Make time for your girlfriends.

Get good at giving inspiring speeches.

Start your own blog and name it
after your favourite Italian tipple.

Learn how to play polo,
the royal sport of choice.

Perfect your Sunday roast.
It's a game changer;
and it will impress the in-laws.

Read *Eat, Pray, Love,* then talk about it on your blog, *a lot.*

Spend a month travelling in Italy
after reading *Eat, Pray, Love.*

Have an estranged family member
write a 'tell all' book about you.

Run. It keeps you fit and improves
your chance of catching a prince,
should one cross your path.

Meditate, it helps focus the mind and means you're more likely to fulfil your dreams (of being a princess).

Make sure your playlist includes
the likes of Crystal Fighters,
Maggie Rogers and Janelle Monáe.

Move into a swanky new apartment
at Kensington Palace.

Become a global ambassador
for World Vision.

Love your food.

Cropped pants in vegan leather
and a cool shirt are the perfect go-to
outfit for almost any occasion.

When travelling, look refined.
Crumpled is *so* not chic!

Hummus, carrots, and chia seed pudding
are your pantry staples!

Believe in fairy tales.

Can't make the ball? Forget the fairy godmother. Facetime is the only way to communicate long distance with your prince.

Don't forget his granny is a queen to him.
No, really, she is!

Make like a warrior princess
and get into combat training.
You'll rock the military look.

Turn your hand to fashion design.

Be a philanthropist.

Break the internet.

Be a star, but don't make fame
your ultimate aim.

Get yourself Googled, a lot!

Be an advocate for gender equality.

Have an A-list BFF like Serena Williams.

Adopt the three 'S's: sassy, self-assured
and sincere; be all of them, in spades.

Always be proud of who you are.

Be prepared to sacrifice anything for love.

Take a chance on fate and
say yes to that blind date.

Be authentic, what you *see* is what you *get*.

Head-to-toe designer gear is *so* last season.
Opt for jeans, preferably ripped at the knee.

Mix it up and make the slightly weird
truly wonderful; a woolly hat and
oversized shades combo, nailed it!

Seasoned starlet and princess-in-waiting rule
number one: know your camera angles.

Keep your public guessing –
a modern princess is never predictable.

Be flexible in body and mind.
Practice yoga to within an inch of your life.

Have Kate Middleton as your sister,
in style, soul and law.

It's all about the superstar smile;
use it, work it, win the nation's heart.

Aspire to the Markle Sparkle;
simply put – just shine.

*Publishing Director* Sarah Lavelle
*Editorial Assistant* Harriet Webster
*Words* Alison Davies
*Designer* Thomas Smith
*Production Controller* Tom Moore
*Production Director* Vincent Smith

First published in 2018 by Quadrille,
an imprint of Hardie Grant Publishing

Quadrille
52-54 Southwark Street
London SE1 1UN

Cataloguing in Publication Data: a catalogue record
for this book is available from the British Library.

ISBN 978 1 78713 262 7

Printed in China